Sanjeev Kapoor's Party Cooking

POPULAR PRAKASHAN PVT. LTD.
301, Mahalaxmi Chambers
22, Bhulabhai Desai Road
Mumbai – 400026.

(4158)
ISBN 978-81-7991-410-6

Design: FourPlus Advertising Pvt Ltd

Photography: Bharat Bhirangi

Food Stylist: Anupa Das

Printed at Saurabh Printers Pvt Ltd,
A-16, Sector 4, NOIDA

And published by Ramdas Bhatkal for
POPULAR PRAKASHAN PVT. LTD.
301, Mahalaxmi Chambers
22, Bhulabhai Desai Road
Mumbai - 400026.

Sanjeev Kapoor's

Party Cooking

In association with
Alyona Kapoor

PopulaR prakashan

www.popularprakashan.com

Sanjeev Kapoor's **Party** Cooking

Author's Note

A party is all about entertaining friends and family. Entertaining is an acquired skill and books like the one you are holding in your hands offer help to both seasoned cooks and novices.

Parties are synonymous with fun, but sometimes the host and hostess cannot enjoy their own party because they are worried that something might go wrong! But let me assure you that guests feel uncomfortable if the host or hostess spends the whole evening in the kitchen. So planning is THE secret of a successful party: from the list, to the invitation, to the menu, the setting and décor.

It is important to remember that your guests should be the focus of any event. The main reason for entertaining is to have a happy and spirited gathering of friends and not an overwhelming display of culinary perfection.

Another important consideration is the budget. We all have those no-expenses-spared occasions that occur in our lives, but those are few; for most of us a party is planned around a budget. It is better to have lots of something seasonal and inexpensive than to serve a meagre platter of something out-of-season and expensive.

Putting together a perfect menu is really a balancing act. You have to combine simple dishes with complex ones, dark-coloured foods with light-coloured ones, sharp and strong flavours with something more subtle and gentle on the palate. Also take into account the time taken to prepare each dish. Don't make every dish complicated and time-consuming or you will get frustrated. Remember there is virtue in simplicity. Don't plan lots of dishes that need last-minute cooking.

After the preparations are done, the kitchen has been wiped clean, the table is sparkling with crockery and matching cutlery, and you are ready with a smile for the first guest to arrive, remember to have a wonderful time at your own party. For if you do, so will your guests.

All recipes are meant to serve four people keeping in mind there are other complementary dishes in the meal. So whether it is a small cosy party for a

select few or a boisterous bash, go ahead and try out the great recipes which lie within these covers. Then, sit back and enjoy the compliments!

Happy Cooking!

Throw a Great Party!

Make those Lists!

• Get ready to make various lists which are absolutely essential for any party. Plan the basics well, including the format of the party, whether it is formal or informal, or a theme party. There are also lists of the guests, menu, ingredients, fun activities, decorations etc.

• Pay special attention to the guest list: your guests should be pleasant company for each other.

• Plan for heavy cleaning, if needed, well ahead of the party. If you need sofas cleaned and glass windows shined, take care of those chores at least a week ahead of time.

• Make an inventory of pots, pans, dishes, cutlery, glasses, napkins, plates, bowls etc. to make sure you have all the equipment you need for cooking and serving. Otherwise, you can borrow some from friends. If it is a kid's party, a teen party, an informal get-together (potluck) for family or friends, buy disposable ware.

• Shop for foods and supplies that can be purchased in advance (like cereals and tinned or bottled food.) Make a list of those foods that need to be bought the week of the party or specially ordered, and last-minute purchases like fresh fruit, vegetables and ice creams.

• Before you go shopping, clean out your refrigerator to make room for all those prepared foods and make-ahead dishes.

Before the Party

• Think about how you want to decorate. Decorations for a party can be as simple as candlesticks on the table, or more elaborate like streamers, balloons, tablecloths, flower arrangements and even chair slipcovers.

• Arrange the furniture so that everyone is within comfortable talking distance. This will help conversation to flow freely. Have sufficient small tables for the guests to rest their glasses. Keep the top of one counter free in the dining area for chaotic dumping of dishes. And keep the crockery flow smooth by clearing it up as often as possible.

• Have one trusted friend 'on call' on the day of the party. If you find that you need anything at the last minute you will have someone who can shop for you on their way to your party.

• Make well-placed and clearly marked areas for garbage or disposable ware.

• Have plenty of ice on hand.

• Always overestimate time required to prepare your dishes.

Food Choices

• Once the dishes that need to be served hot are cooked, transfer them into microwavable serving bowls or platters, so they can be popped into the microwave just before serving. This will enable you to wash the cooking utensils before the party so that

there is less to wash up once the party is over.

• As far as possible, don't repeat a main ingredient. For example, don't serve a prawn appetiser and a main dish with prawns.

• Consider the colours of the food that will be served together and make sure there is variety. Colours and textures of the various dishes should complement each other.

• Offer both hot and cold foods on a buffet.

• One of the worst mistakes a hostess can make is to plan a menu that requires her to be in the kitchen cooking throughout her party. Plan a menu that can be almost completely cooked in advance and simply re-heated when your guests arrive. Have no more than two recipes (one is even better), that need last minute preparation. If you cook the foods you love, your guests will love it too.

• Provide guests with non-alcoholic drink choices.

• Assume some of your guests will be vegetarians. Check with your guests ahead of time for food allergies or religious or health food restrictions.

• Always prepare a selection of items that can be served at room temperature. That way you do not have to worry about hot starters getting cold, or your cold desserts melting.

Cleaning Up

• Trust large garbage bags to do the dirty work! They are the handiest things to have around when the party is over!

• Make the art of giving away leftovers classy. Have clear plastic containers filled up and labelled with the names of the dishes which you can offer your guests as they leave. It is a graceful way of inviting guests to select what they would like to carry home.

• For dirty dishes, place a strong carton or large plastic container near the counter in the kitchen. Put used crockery and cutlery into it till you wash up directly after the party if you have the energy. If you are going to postpone the washing up to the next day, soak all the crockery in soapy water in the plastic container or the kitchen sink till the following morning. At least the counters will be tidy and free from clutter.

• Tidy up the party room and the house before going to bed. Move everything that needs to be tackled into one room: either the dining room or the kitchen. You will be less stressed the following morning with the knowledge that only one room needs your attention!

Acknowledgements

Afsheen Panjwani

Anjali Sawant

Anupa Das

Ashwini Patwardhan

Bharati Anand

Harpal Singh Sokhi

Jayadeep Chaubal

Jayanthi Mahalingam

Jyotsna & Mayur Dvivedi

Mrs. Lata & Capt. K. K. Lohana

Namrata & Sanjiv Bahl

Neena Murdeshwar

Puja & Rajeev Kapoor

Rajeev Matta

Rita D'Souza

Sanjay Thorat

Saurabh Mishra

Shilpa Rane

Smeeta Bhatkal

Swapnil Naik

Tripta Bhagattjee

Vinayak Gawande

Sanjeev Kapoor's **Party** Cooking

C o n t e n t s

Party Punch

Ingredients

4 tbsp	rose syrup
2 cups	orange juice
2 cups	mango juice
4 scoops	vanilla ice cream
1 cup	ice cubes

Method

1 Pour one tablespoon of rose syrup into each glass and swirl to form a design. Place the glasses in the refrigerator to chill.

2 Process the orange juice, mango juice and vanilla ice cream with the ice cubes in a blender till smooth.

3 Pour the prepared punch into the rose syrup-lined glasses and serve immediately.

Note: Pretty drinks all in a row... eyes will light up at the sight of a tray lined up with glasses of this colourful beverage.

Chocolate-Coffee Ambrosia

Ingredients

3 cups	milk
4 tsp	instant coffee powder
4 tbsp	sugar
4 scoops	vanilla ice cream
4 tbsp	advocaat (liqueur)

Method

1 Heat the milk and set aside.

2 To make the coffee, combine the coffee powder and sugar in a large bowl. Add two to three tablespoons of water and whisk for six to eight minutes till the mixture changes colour and turns creamy.

3 Pour the mixture into four large cups. Strain the milk and pour into the cups till three- fourths full and stir gently.

4 Gently place a scoop of ice cream on the coffee in each cup. Drizzle a tablespoon of advocaat over the ice cream and serve immediately.

....

Note: Dinner is over and your guests are replete. Bring on one more surprise with this advocaat-laced delight that is truly creamy and soothing. It can be served warm without the ice cream.

Virgin Pina Colada

Ingredients

1¾ cups	unsweetened pineapple (ananas) juice
8 tbsp	thick coconut milk
8 tbsp	shredded tender coconut flesh
2 cups	vanilla ice cream
	crushed ice
8 tbsp	chopped pineapple (ananas) chunks
16-20	tinned cherries

Method

1 Process the pineapple juice, coconut milk, coconut, vanilla ice cream and ice in a blender till smooth.

2 Pour immediately into individual Collins glasses or tender coconut shells. Serve, decorated with pineapple chunks and cherries.

Note: All the tropical flavours true to the legendary rum-based drink minus the alcohol! The sweetness of the coconut milk blends with the sourness of the pineapple and every sip makes one marvel at the combination. Rarely will your guests refuse seconds!

Cream Of Asparagus And Almond Soup

Ingredients

300 g	asparagus (shatavari)
10-12	almonds (badam)
	Salt to taste
2 tbsp	butter
1	medium onion, chopped
2 tbsp	refined flour (maida)
2½ cups	Vegetable Stock (below)
4-5	black peppercorns (kali mirch), crushed
2	cups milk

Vegetable stock

Place 1 sliced onion, 1 sliced carrot, one 2-3 inch celery stalk, 2 garlic cloves, 1 bay leaf, 5-6 black peppercorns and 2-3 cloves in a pan with five cups of water and bring to a boil. Simmer for 15 minutes and strain.

Method

1 Trim the asparagus, discarding the woody part of the stem. Cut the remainder into short lengths, reserving a few tips for garnishing. Blanch the reserved tips in boiling salted water for one or two minutes. Drain and refresh in cold water.

2 Blanch the remaining asparagus in boiling water for two to three minutes. Drain and refresh in cold water. Purée in a blender.

3 Broil or dry-roast the almonds over a medium heat till the skins change colour slightly. Remove from heat, cool and slice into slivers.

4 Melt the butter in a pan and add the onion. Sauté over a low heat until soft. Stir in the flour and cook for one minute, then gradually add the stock and whisk so that no lumps are formed. Bring the mixture to a boil.

5 Simmer for two to three minutes until thickened, then stir in the asparagus purée, salt and crushed peppercorns.

6 Add the milk and simmer for two to three minutes, stirring continuously.

7 Serve hot, garnished with the blanched asparagus tips and almond slivers.

Note: This jade-coloured soup is a great appetiser. I suggest you do not make it too much ahead of time as it is best served freshly made.

Mushroom Cappuccino

Ingredients

15 large	fresh button mushrooms, thickly sliced
1 tbsp	butter
1	bay leaf (tej patta)
1	small onion, chopped
4-6	garlic cloves, chopped
4 cups	Vegetable Stock (page 18)
	Salt to taste
¼ tsp	white pepper powder
¾ cup	cream
2 cups	milk, chilled
1 tsp	cinnamon (dalchini) powder

Method

1 Melt the butter in a heavy-bottomed pan. Add the bay leaf, onion and garlic and sauté for two to three minutes or till onion is translucent.

2 Add the mushrooms and sauté for one minute. Add one cup of vegetable stock and cook for five more minutes. Remove from heat and cool. Remove bay leaf and discard.

3 Make a purée of the cooked mushrooms and add the remaining vegetable stock. Return to heat and bring to a boil. Add salt and white pepper powder, lower the heat and simmer for two to three minutes.

4 Stir in the cream and remove from heat. Pour the soup into individual cups and keep warm.

5 Pour the chilled milk into a chilled bowl. Beat with a fork till it develops a thick froth. Collect the froth with a ladle and place on the hot mushroom soup giving it a cappuccino effect.

6 Sprinkle cinnamon powder and serve immediately.

Note: I once surprised my guests by serving this soup in large coffee mugs while they were having their starters. They actually thought coffee was being served and were reluctant to help themselves to a mug till I clarified!

Chef's Tip : Use milk with a high fat content for a thick froth.

Smoked Chicken And Fruit Salad

225 g	boneless chicken breasts
	Salt to taste
2 tsp	lemon juice
75 g	seedless green grapes,
	peeled and halved
1	pear (naspati),
	peeled, cored and sliced
25 g	walnut (akhrot) halves
4	iceberg lettuce leaves, shredded
2	celery stalks, chopped
1	red capsicum (lal Shimla mirch), sliced

Dressing

2 tbsp	yogurt (dahi)
2 tbsp	Mayonnaise (page 36)
2 tbsp	grated cucumber
1 tsp	grated onion
½ tsp	chopped fresh tarragon
	Salt to taste
	Black pepper (kali mirch) powder to
	taste

To garnish

A few fresh tarragon sprigs

1 Marinate the chicken breasts with salt and lemon juice for about half an hour. Grill till both sides are evenly cooked and golden. Set aside to cool. Cut into strips.

2 In a large bowl, combine the chicken strips with the grapes, pear, walnuts, lettuce, celery and capsicum.

3 In a separate bowl, combine the yogurt, mayonnaise, cucumber, onion, tarragon, salt and pepper.

4 Just before serving, spoon the dressing over the salad ingredients and toss well to mix.

5 Garnish with a few sprigs of fresh tarragon and serve.

Note: I suggest that you grill the chicken much ahead of time, as all you will have to do later is toss everything with the dressing. Take your time over the grilling as the chicken has to cook through.

Summer Tomato Pasta Salad

Ingredients

10-12	cherry tomatoes, halved
1½ cups	penne (quill-shaped pasta)
	Salt to taste
¼	medium broccoli, separated into small florets
½ tsp	sugar
10-12	black peppercorns (kali mirch)
15-20	basil leaves (tulsi ke patte)
2 tbsp	olive oil
150 g	cottage cheese (paneer), cut into 2-inch long strips
1 tbsp	vinegar (sirka)
1 tsp	caster sugar
2 tbsp	pine nuts (chilgoze) or chopped walnuts (akhrot) optional

Method

1 Cook the pasta in five to six cups of boiling salted water till *al dente* (cooked, but still firm to the bite). Drain, refresh in cold water and spread on a large plate to cool.

2 Boil the broccoli with salt and sugar for two to three minutes. Drain, refresh in cold water and set aside.

3 Reserve 3-4 basil leaves for garnishing and crush the rest with the peppercorns and one tablespoon of olive oil with a mortar and pestle. Stir the remaining olive oil into the paste.

4 In a large bowl, combine the pasta, cherry tomatoes, broccoli, *paneer*, prepared paste, vinegar, caster sugar and salt. Toss well to mix.

5 Transfer the salad to a serving dish, garnish with the remaining basil leaves and pine nuts or walnuts and serve immediately.

Note: They say eat with your eyes first! This salad will whet your appetite — with the white of the pasta, the red tomato and the green broccoli it is a visual delight. The paneer is an Indian touch that I just could not resist!.

Chef's Tip: You can also use large tomatoes cut into quarters in place of cherry tomatoes.

Red Onion, Tomato And Pasta Salad

Ingredients

1	large red onion, thinly sliced
4	medium tomatoes, quartered and seeded
3 cups	short pasta in different shapes
1	yellow capsicum (pili Shimla mirch), roasted
2	small zucchini, sliced
	Salt to taste
	A few sprigs of fresh basil (tulsi ke patte), to garnish

Dressing

4 tbsp	olive oil
1½ tbsp	red wine vinegar
1 tsp	Dijon mustard
½ tsp	caster sugar
	Salt to taste
12-15	black peppercorns (kali mirch), crushed
½ cup	roughly torn fresh basil leaves (tulsi ke patte)

Method

1 Cook the pasta in boiling salted water till *al dente* (cooked, but still firm to the bite).

2 Cool the capsicum, peel and slice into strips. Blanch the zucchini and refresh in cold water.

3 Mix together all the ingredients for the dressing.

4 Drain the pasta well and transfer to a large serving bowl. Add the dressing and toss well. Add the capsicum, zucchini, onion and tomatoes; toss well to mix.

5 Cover the bowl and leave to stand at room temperature for about thirty minutes to allow the flavours to develop.

6 Serve, garnished with sprigs of basil.

Note: This is a desi kachumber made extraordinary with exotic vegetables and pasta. It is a novelty and is so colourful that even kids will go for it!

Caesar Salad

2	thick slices of bread
1 tbsp	oil
2	garlic cloves, peeled and roughly crushed
½	bunch (135 g) iceberg lettuce
½	bunch (100 g) lollo rosso
5-6	basil leaves (tulsi ke patte)
100 g	Parmesan cheese, shaved or grated

Dressing

2	eggs
1 tsp	French mustard paste
1 tsp	Worcestershire sauce
2 tbsp	extra virgin olive oil
	Salt to taste
3-4	black peppercorns (kali mirch), crushed

1 Cut the bread into one-inch cubes.

2 Heat the oil in a pan and add the garlic. Add the bread cubes and sauté till slightly crisp and browned at the edges. Remove and set aside.

3 Wash and tear the lettuce leaves roughly and place in a large bowl. Tear basil leaves and add to the lettuce. Add the cheese shavings or grated cheese.

4 Boil sufficient water in a pan; add the eggs and boil for two to three minutes only.

5 Break the lightly boiled eggs into a separate bowl and whisk well. Add the mustard paste, Worcestershire sauce, olive oil, salt and freshly crushed peppercorns and whisk till well blended.

6 Add the fried bread and toss lightly. Pour the dressing over the salad and toss lightly. Serve immediately.

Note: You may come across different versions of Caesar Salad in various hotels and restaurants. This is my favourite and was served in my friend's restaurant in Wellington, New Zealand.

Chef's Tip: Use a vegetable peeler to shave cheese into wafer-thin slices.

Chimichangas

Tortillas
1¼ cups +1 tbsp	refined flour (maida), sifted
2 tbsp	oil + for deep-frying
½ tsp	salt
1	egg, beaten

Filling
3 tbsp	oil
10-12	garlic cloves, chopped
1	small onion, chopped
4-5	French beans, diced
1	small carrot, diced
¼ cup	corn kernels (makai ke dane)
	Salt to taste
1 tsp	red chilli flakes
½ tsp	paprika
300 g	boneless chicken, boiled and chopped
2 tbsp	grated processed cheese

1 To make the filling, heat the oil in a pan and sauté the garlic and onion. Add the French beans, carrot and corn; toss and add the salt, chilli flakes and paprika.

2 Add the chicken and toss well to mix. Cook for one minute, remove from heat and set aside to cool. When slightly cool, add the grated cheese and mix well.

3 For the tortillas, mix together the flour, two tablespoons oil, salt and enough water to make a stiff dough. Rest the dough for fifteen minutes, covered with a damp cloth. Divide the dough into eight portions and shape into balls.

4 Mix together the egg and one tablespoon of flour to make a smooth mixture.

5 Roll out each portion of dough into a thin round, dusting with flour as required.

6 Heat a *tawa* and cook each tortilla lightly on both sides. Do not cook completely.

7 To assemble the chimichangas, place each tortilla on a plate. Place two spoons of filling in the centre and roll up. Seal the ends with the egg mixture.

8 Heat plenty of oil in a *kadai* and deep-fry the chimichangas till crisp and golden brown. Drain on absorbent paper.

9 Slice diagonally and serve hot with sweet chilli sauce or tomato ketchup.

....

Note: You can make a vegetarian version by substituting chicken with either tofu, paneer or soya nuggets. Tastes wonderful!

Chicken And Spinach Pizzas

Ingredients

2	eight-inch pizza breads
300 g	minced chicken (keema)
1	medium bunch fresh spinach (palak), chopped
2 tbsp	olive oil
1	large onion, chopped
4-5	garlic cloves, chopped
¼ tsp	dried mixed herbs
1 tsp	red chilli flakes
2	large tomatoes, blanched and chopped
	Salt to taste
¼ cup	tomato purée

Topping

2 cups	grated mozzarella cheese
2 tsp	red chilli flakes
1 tsp	dried oregano
4 tsp	olive oil

Method

1 Preheat the oven to 220°C/425°F/Gas Mark 7.

2 For the sauce, heat the olive oil in a pan; add the onion and garlic and stir-fry for a few minutes. Add the mixed herbs, chilli flakes and chicken mince and sauté over a medium heat for two to three minutes.

3 Add the tomatoes and salt, sauté for a minute, cover and cook over a low heat till done. Add the spinach and continue to cook for another two minutes.

4 Add the tomato purée, stir, adjust the seasoning and simmer for two to three minutes till the sauce attains a thick dropping consistency. Remove from heat and set aside.

5 Spread the sauce on the pizza bread and top with the grated mozzarella cheese. Sprinkle chilli flakes and oregano and drizzle olive oil on top. Place the pizzas on a greased baking tray and bake till the cheese melts and starts bubbling.

6 Remove from the oven, cut into six or eight wedges each and serve hot.

Note: You can use mini pizza breads for this recipe. I once served bite-size pizzas: I took a cookie cutter and stamped out shapes from large pizza breads. A great hit!

Crusty Potato Fingers

2	large potatoes
2½ cups	cornflakes, crushed
	Oil for deep-frying

Batter

1	onion, roughly chopped
1	green chilli, chopped
½ inch	ginger
	Salt to taste
½ cup	refined flour (maida)
1 tbsp	cornflour

Method

1 Peel and cut the potatoes lengthways into even strips. Grind the onion, green chilli, ginger and salt to a fine paste.

2 Mix the ground paste with the flour and cornflour. Add two tablespoons of water to make a thick batter.

3 Heat four cups of water in a pan. Add the salt and parboil the sliced potatoes. Drain and set aside.

4 Heat plenty of oil in a *kadai*. Dip the potatoes in the batter, roll in crushed cornflakes and deep-fry till golden. Drain on absorbent paper.

5 Serve hot, with sauce or chutney.

Note: You can also cut the potatoes into large cubes. In which case, serve them on toothpicks.

Savoury Crispies With Creamy Onion Dip

Ingredients

2	pita breads

Onion dip

2	medium onions, sliced
	Oil for deep-frying
¾ cup	Mayonnaise (below)
2 tbsp	cream
1	stalk spring onion greens (hare pyaaz ke patte), chopped
	Salt to taste
1 tsp	black peppercorns (kali mirch), crushed

Method

1 Slice the pita bread horizontally and cut again into long triangular slices.

2 Heat a *tawa* and arrange the pita slices on it. Toast both sides over a low heat till crisp.

3 Heat the oil in a *kadai* and deep-fry the onions till golden brown. Drain on absorbent paper. Crush the fried onions lightly.

4 Combine the mayonnaise, cream, spring onion greens, salt, crushed peppercorns and browned onions. Place in a refrigerator to chill for half an hour.

5 Serve the pita crispies with the onion dip.

Mayonnaise

Place 1 egg yolk, salt to taste, ¼ tsp each white pepper powder, mustard powder and sugar and 1 tsp vinegar in a clean bowl and mix thoroughly with a whisk.

Alternatively, process the mixture in a blender.
Add 1 cup of oil, a little at a time, whisking or blending continuously, until all the oil is incorporated.
Add 1 tsp lemon juice and adjust seasoning.
Store in an airtight jar in the refrigerator.

Note: Finger foods sometimes surprise us with their simplicity. The difference in this recipe is that the onions are fried producing a strongly-flavoured dip which is perfect with plain pita.

Paneer Ke Tinke

Ingredients

300 g	cottage cheese (paneer), cut into 1-inch pieces
1 tsp	oil+ for shallow-frying
2 tbsp	gram flour (besan)
¾ cup	drained (hung) yogurt (chakka)
1 tsp	roasted cumin (bhuna jeera) powder
3-4	black peppercorns (kali mirch), crushed
½ tsp	roasted crushed dried fenugreek leaves (kasuri methi)
½ tsp	turmeric powder (haldi)
½ tsp	garam masala powder
5 tsp	lemon juice
	Salt to taste
	A few saffron threads (kesar), optional
1	medium onion, cut into 1-inch pieces
1	medium green capsicum (hari Shimla mirch), cut into1-inch pieces
1	medium red capsicum (lal Shimla mirch), cut into 1-inch pieces
6	satay sticks

Method

1 Heat one teaspoon of oil in a pan and roast the gram flour over a low heat till fragrant.

2 Combine the yogurt, cumin powder, peppercorns, *kasuri methi*, turmeric powder, *garam masala* powder, lemon juice, salt and saffron in a bowl and mix well. Add the roasted gram flour and mix well. Add the *paneer* and toss gently. Set aside to marinate for ten to fifteen minutes.

3 Separate the layers of the cut onion. Thread the ingredients in the following order onto the satay sticks: onion, *paneer*, green capsicum, red capsicum, *paneer* and finally onion.

4 Heat a shallow pan, drizzle some oil and place the satay sticks on it. Cook turning the satay sticks from time to time so that the *paneer* pieces are cooked evenly on all sides.

5 Serve hot with mint chutney.

Mint chutney

Grind 5 cups mint leaves, 3 cups coriander leaves, 10 green chillies, 3 onions, and 3 inches of ginger to a fine paste, adding a little water if required. Stir in 1 tablespoon lemon juice, salt and pomegranate seed (anardana) powder.

....

Note: Attractive food breaks the ice at any party and starters set the pace... paneer *on sticks will definitely do wonders.*

Mini Falafel Burgers

Ingredients

1 cup	chickpeas (kabuli chana), soaked overnight
2-3	garlic cloves, chopped
2 tbsp	chopped fresh coriander (hara dhania)
2 tbsp	chopped fresh parsley (ajmoda)
4-5	stalks spring onion greens (hare pyaaz ke patte), chopped
¼ cup	breadcrumbs
	A small pinch of soda bicarbonate
½ tsp	roasted cumin (bhuna jeera) powder
	Salt to taste
¼ tsp	black pepper (kali mirch) powder
½ tsp	paprika
	Oil for deep-frying

Yogurt sauce

½ cup	drained (hung) yogurt (chakka)
2 tbsp	cream
1 tbsp	chopped fresh coriander (hara dhania)
3-4	garlic cloves, chopped
1 tsp	chopped fresh parsley (ajmoda)
	Salt to taste
½ tbsp	lemon juice

To serve

1	medium unpeeled cucumber, sliced into ribbons
8	mini burger buns
	Butter, as required
4	lettuce leaves, halved
2	cheese slices, quartered
1	medium cucumber, sliced
1	large tomato, sliced

Method

1 Drain the chickpeas and spread on a kitchen towel to dry. Process the chickpeas along with garlic, coriander, parsley, spring onion greens and breadcrumbs in a food processor to a coarse mixture.

2 Add the soda bicarbonate and cumin powder and mix well. Season with salt, pepper and paprika. Knead the mixture well and place in a refrigerator to chill for a couple of hours.

3 Shape tablespoons full of the chilled mixture into round patties. Arrange on a greased plate and place in a refrigerator till ready to fry.

4 Heat plenty of oil in a *kadai* and deep-fry the falafels till golden brown. Drain on absorbent paper.

5 Mix together all the ingredients for the yogurt sauce and chill till required.

6 Apply salt to the cucumber ribbons and set aside.

7 Cut the burger buns in half and spread the cut sides with butter.

8 On the bottom half of each bun place a lettuce leaf, a quartered cheese slice, cucumber slice and tomato slice.

9 Place a fried falafel on the vegetable slices and top with yogurt sauce and cucumber ribbons. Cover with the top half of the bun. Serve immediately.

Note: A great hit with kids and adults alike! The yogurt sauce can be served separately as a dip with a variety of crudités so you can make large batches of it.

Chef's Tip: In place of mini burgers you can also use small round buns.

Mini Tostadas

Ingredients

12	ready-made corn tostadas
	A few iceberg lettuce leaves, torn into bite-sized pieces
1 tbsp	pomegranate (anar) kernels
	A few sprigs of fresh parsley (ajmoda)

Salsa

½ cup	corn kernels (makai ke dane)
1 tbsp	olive oil
1	medium onion, chopped
1	medium green capsicum (hari Shimla mirch), cut into small pieces
1	medium red capsicum (lal Shimla mirch), cut into small pieces
1	medium yellow capsicum (pili Shimla mirch), cut into small pieces
50 g	cottage cheese (paneer), cut into small pieces
7-8	black peppercorns (kali mirch), crushed
¼ tsp	paprika
1 tbsp	chopped fresh coriander (hara dhania)
	Salt to taste
1 tbsp	lemon juice
1 tbsp	balsamic vinegar (sirka), optional

Method

1 For the salsa, roast the corn in a pan over a high heat to scorch the kernels lightly. Add the olive oil and onion and sauté till translucent. Remove from heat and transfer to a bowl. Set aside to cool.

2 Place the capsicums and cottage cheese in a separate bowl. Add the crushed peppercorns, paprika, fresh coriander, salt and lemon juice and mix well.

3 Add the sautéed corn and balsamic vinegar. Adjust salt and toss to mix.

4 To assemble, place the tostadas on a plate and place a piece of lettuce leaf on each. Spoon some salsa on each tostada.

5 Garnish with pomegranate kernels and parsley sprigs and serve immediately.

Note: A saviour for large unplanned parties... looks excellent and requires minimum effort!

Chef's Tip: Ready-made tostadas are easily available in the market.

Parsi Mutton Cutlets

Ingredients

500 g	minced mutton (keema)
5	slices bread
	Salt to taste
½ tbsp	ginger paste
½ tbsp	garlic paste
6-8	green chillies, finely chopped
1½ tsp	red chilli powder
1 tsp	coriander (dhania) powder
1 tsp	roasted cumin (bhuna jeera) powder
¼ tsp	turmeric powder (haldi)
2 tbsp	chopped fresh mint (pudina)
2 tbsp	chopped fresh coriander (hara dhania)
1 cup	breadcrumbs
	Oil for deep-frying
4	eggs
	Lemon wedges
	Onion rings

Method

1 Squeeze the minced mutton between your palms to remove excess water.

2 Soak the bread in one cup of water for half a minute and squeeze to remove excess water.

3 Place the mutton, bread, salt, ginger paste, garlic paste, green chillies, chilli powder, coriander powder, cumin powder, turmeric powder, chopped fresh mint and coriander in a deep bowl. Mix well and set aside to marinate for three to four hours, preferably in a refrigerator.

4 Divide the marinated mince into twelve equal portions; shape each portion into a ball and roll in breadcrumbs. Place each ball on a flat surface and flatten with your fingers into a four-inch patty, dusting with breadcrumbs. Place the cutlets in a refrigerator for half an hour.

5 Heat plenty of oil in a deep *kadai*.

6 Beat the eggs lightly with salt and two tablespoons of water. Dip the cutlets in the egg and deep-fry for two to three minutes on each side. Drain on absorbent paper.

7 Serve hot with lemon wedges and onion rings.

Note: These cutlets can be made a day ahead and frozen. Place butter paper between the layers and fry as you need them.

Fish Tikka Achaari

Ingredients

2	surmai fillets (400 g), cut into 2-inch pieces
2 tbsp	lemon juice
	Salt to taste
1 tsp	garlic paste
1 tsp	ginger paste
½ tsp	turmeric powder (haldi)
2 tsp	Kashmiri chilli powder
1 tsp	mustard seeds (rai)
1 tsp	fennel seeds (saunf)
1 tsp	onion seeds (kalonji)
½ tsp	fenugreek seeds (methi dana)
½ tsp	black salt
2 tbsp	mustard oil (rai ka tel)
1 cup	yogurt (dahi), whisked
4 tbsp	butter, melted

Green chutney

Grind together 1 cup fresh coriander leaves, ½ cup fresh mint leaves, 2-3 green chillies, black salt to taste, ¼ teaspoon sugar and 1 tablespoon lemon juice to a smooth paste using a little water if required.

Method

1 Place the fish in a bowl; add the lemon juice, salt, garlic paste, ginger paste, turmeric powder and chilli powder and mix well.

2 Heat a pan and dry-roast the mustard seeds, fennel seeds, onion seeds and fenugreek seeds. Add the black salt and crush with a mortar and pestle.

3 Heat the mustard oil in a pan to smoking point; remove from heat and set aside to cool.

4 Add the yogurt to the fish along with the crushed spices and mix. Leave to marinate for thirty minutes.

5 Preheat the oven to 200°C/400°F/Gas Mark 6.

6 Add the cooled mustard oil to the marinated fish and mix.

7 Place the fish on a greased rack in an oven tray. Baste with butter and cook for ten to fifteen minutes or till done.

8 Serve hot with green chutney.

Note: This is one of my favourite things and I enjoy making this tikka as much as I enjoy eating it. As the flavours are quite strong, be ready with some good palate cleansers like vegetable crudités to follow.

Chef's Tip: If you do not have an oven, you can skewer the fish pieces on satay sticks and cook on a non-stick tawa.

Pan-fried Mushrooms

Ingredients

20-24	fresh button mushrooms, quartered
½ cup	porcini mushrooms (optional)
½ cup	oyster mushrooms (optional)
1	small red capsicum (lal Shimla mirch), cut into ½-inch pieces
1	small yellow capsicum (pili Shimla mirch), cut into ½-inch pieces
1 tbsp	olive oil
2	medium onions, cut into ½-inch cubes
3	garlic cloves, crushed
1 tbsp	soy sauce
1 tbsp	red chilli sauce
½ tbsp	vinegar (sirka)
½ tsp	dried thyme
	Salt to taste
8-10	black peppercorns (kali mirch), crushed
7-8	fresh basil leaves (tulsi ke patte), roughly torn

Method

1 If using porcini and oyster mushrooms, soak in lukewarm water for twenty minutes. Drain. Wash well and set aside.

2 Heat the oil in a large pan. Add the onions and sauté over a medium heat till translucent. Add garlic and stir-fry for a minute.

3 Add the mushrooms and red and yellow capsicum and sauté over a high heat for three minutes.

4 Add the soy sauce, chilli sauce and vinegar and sauté for another two minutes.

5 Add the thyme, salt and crushed peppercorns. Remove from heat, stir in the basil and serve hot.

Note: Mushroom lovers are going to lap this one up. A visual delight, this stir-fried treat will definitely add more grace to your party table.

Ratatouille

Ingredients

2	medium long variety of eggplants (baingan)
2	medium zucchini
	Salt to taste
1 tbsp	olive oil
2	medium onions, sliced into rings
4 tbsp	tomato purée
4	garlic cloves, chopped
2	medium green capsicums (hari Shimla mirch), cut into thin strips
3	medium tomatoes, blanched, peeled, seeded and chopped
¼ tsp	coriander (dhania) powder
	A pinch of cinnamon (dalchini) powder
	A few basil leaves (tulsi ke patte), shredded
	White pepper powder to taste

Method

1 Halve the eggplants and zucchinis lengthways. Cut them again into thick slices. Place the eggplant in a colander and sprinkle with salt. Place a weighted plate on top and leave to drain for one hour.

2 Heat the olive oil in a non-stick pan; add the onion and sauté over a low heat until translucent. Stir in the tomato purée and cook over a medium heat for three to four minutes, stirring occasionally.

3 Rinse the salted eggplants and drain well. Add with the sliced zucchini to the pan. Add the garlic and capsicums and simmer for about five minutes.

4 Add the tomatoes, coriander powder, cinnamon powder, basil, salt and white pepper powder. Stir once or twice and cook over a medium heat for about ten minutes, stirring frequently.

5 Adjust the seasoning and serve hot.

Note: Pronounced 'ra-ta-tou-ee', this is a French stew which uses colourful vegetables to maximum advantage. Serve with crusty bread.

Potato Cheese Balls In Spinach Gravy

Ingredients

2	medium potatoes, boiled and mashed
200 g	cottage cheese (paneer), mashed
3 tbsp	cornflour
½ tsp	red chilli powder
½ inch	ginger, chopped
	Salt to taste
½ tsp	white pepper powder
12-15	cashew nuts (kaju), chopped
12-15	raisins (kishmish)
	Oil for deep-frying

Spinach gravy

2	medium bunches (500 g) fresh spinach leaves (palak)
2	green chillies, chopped
3 tbsp	oil
½ tsp	caraway seeds (shahi jeera)
5-6	garlic cloves, chopped
½ cup	tomato purée
½ tsp	turmeric powder (haldi)
1 tsp	coriander (dhania) powder
1 tsp	garam masala powder
¼ cup	cream

Method

1 Mix together the mashed potatoes and *paneer*, cornflour, chilli powder, ginger, salt and white pepper powder. Divide the mixture into sixteen balls. Stuff each ball with cashew nuts and raisins.

2 Heat plenty of oil in a *kadai* and deep-fry the balls, a few at a time, until golden brown. Drain on absorbent paper and set aside.

3 For the gravy, blanch the spinach in plenty of water; refresh under cold running water and drain well. Blend with the green chillies to a smooth purée.

4 Heat the oil in a *handi*; add the caraway seeds and garlic and stir-fry for a few minutes. Add the spinach purée and cook for about two to three minutes. Stir in the tomato purée and mix well.

5 Add the turmeric powder, coriander powder and salt. Stir and cook for four to five minutes.

6 Add one cup of water and bring to a boil. Lower the heat and simmer for five to seven minutes. Stir in the *garam masala* powder and cook till the curry is reduced by half. Lower the heat, stir in the cream and cook for half a minute. Remove from heat.

7 Arrange the *koftas* in a serving dish. Pour the hot gravy over and serve hot.

*Note: Make the **koftas** and the gravy ahead of time. The last minute putting together is what makes this dish so perfect for a party! I sometimes halve the **koftas** and serve them cut side up so that the stuffing can be seen.*

Spinach And Mozzarella Lasagne

Ingredients

2	medium bunches (500 g) spinach (palak)
2 tbsp	olive oil
1	medium onion, finely chopped
4	garlic cloves, crushed
4	large tomatoes, blanched, seeded and roughly chopped
	Salt to taste
5-6	black peppercorns (kali mirch), roasted and crushed
½ cup	grated mozzarella cheese
½ cup	grated processed cheese

Fresh lasagne

1 cup	refined flour (maida)
1 tbsp	olive oil
2	egg yolks

White sauce

2 tbsp	refined flour (maida)
2 tbsp	butter
2 cups	warm milk
	Salt to taste
	White pepper powder to taste

Garnish

2 tbsp	chopped fresh parsley (ajmoda)

Method

1 Blanch the spinach and refresh under running water. Drain in a colander and squeeze to remove excess water. Chop coarsely.

2 Heat the oil in a pan; add the onion and garlic and cook until the onion has softened slightly. Add the spinach and cook till quite dry. Add the tomatoes and cook for about two minutes. Season with salt and crushed peppercorns and set aside.

3 Sift the flour and one-fourth teaspoon salt together. Make a well in the centre and pour in the olive oil and mix into the flour. Add the egg yolks and knead into a moderately hard dough. Knead lightly for five to ten minutes. Cover the dough with a damp cloth and set aside for ten minutes.

4 Divide the dough into three parts and roll out on a floured board into twelve-inch squares. Cut each square into six-inch wide strips and cook in four cups of boiling salted water for three minutes. Drain the strips and immerse in cold water.

5 Preheat the oven to 200°C/400°F/Gas Mark 6.

6 To make the white sauce, melt the butter in a heavy-bottomed pan and add the flour. Cook for two to three minutes over a low heat till fragrant.

7 Add the warm milk, whisking vigorously to prevent lumps from forming. Add salt and white pepper powder and cook for four to five minutes till the sauce thickens. Pass the sauce through a sieve.

8 In a greased seven-inch square ovenproof dish, spread two to three tablespoons of white sauce at the bottom. Arrange layers of lasagne sheets and spinach mixture alternately, ending with pasta as the top layer.

9 Pour the remaining white sauce over the top layer of pasta and sprinkle mozzarella cheese and processed cheese. Bake for about twenty minutes or till pale gold on top.

10 Cut into squares and serve hot, garnished with parsley.

Chef's Tip: To save time and effort, buy ready-made lasagne sheets which are easily available.

Note: The secret of serving this lasagne is to cut it up into neat square portions. Italians would ideally serve it with a shaker filled with grated Parmesan to add that extra bite to the topping.

Paneer Kaliya

Ingredients

500 g	cottage cheese (paneer), cut into 1-inch cubes
½ cup	almonds (badam), blanched, peeled and ground
2 tbsp	pure ghee
4	green cardamoms (chhoti elaichi)
4	cloves (laung)
10	black peppercorns (kali mirch)
1 inch	cinnamon (dalchini)
2	medium onions, sliced
1 inch	ginger, chopped
2 tbsp	coriander seeds (dhania)
½ tsp	turmeric powder (haldi)
	Salt to taste
2 tbsp	chopped fresh coriander (hara dhania)

Method

1 Heat one tablespoon *ghee* in a *kadai*. Crush the cardamoms, cloves and peppercorns with a mortar and pestle and add to the *ghee*. Add cinnamon and onions and sauté for two to three minutes.

2 Add the ginger and coriander seeds and sauté for a minute longer. Remove from heat, cool slightly and grind into a fine paste with one tablespoon of water.

3 Heat the remaining *ghee* in a pan; add the ground *masala* paste and sauté until the *ghee* separates. Add one tablespoon of water to prevent scorching.

4 Mix the almond paste with one cup of water and add to the *masala*. Add the turmeric powder and simmer for a while. Add salt to taste and mix well.

5 Add the *paneer* cubes and simmer for ten minutes. Serve hot, garnished with chopped fresh coriander.

....

Note: Paneer *dishes have always been considered as something special in most homes. This recipe is enriched with almonds which makes it perfect for special occasions. And when you reveal that it is based on the art of ancient cooking when chillies were not yet in use, it will become a conversation piece!*

Massaman Tofu Curry

Ingredients

400 g	tofu (bean curd), cubed
3 tbsp	Massaman Curry Paste (recipe below)
1 tbsp	oil
1 tbsp	soy sauce
1 tbsp	lemon juice
2 tbsp	roasted peanuts (bhune moongphali)
	Salt to taste

Method

1. Heat the oil in a pan; add the tofu and sauté for a few minutes.

2. Stir in the soy sauce, lemon juice and roasted peanuts.

3. Add the curry paste and salt to taste and mix well.

4. Cook for another fifteen minutes and serve hot.

Massaman curry paste

Ingredients

4	spring onions, finely chopped
12	garlic cloves, chopped
1 inch	galangal, chopped
1	lemon grass stalk, chopped
2	cloves
1 tbsp	coriander seeds (dhania)
1 tsp	cumin seeds (jeera)
5	black peppercorns (kali mirch)
3	dried red chillies, soaked and chopped
1 tsp	salt
1 tsp	shrimp paste (optional)

Method

1. Cook the spring onions, garlic, galangal, lemon grass, cloves, coriander seeds and cumin seeds in a wok over a low heat for about five minutes. Grind to a paste.

2. Add the peppercorns, red chillies and salt and grind again. Add the shrimp paste and grind once more.

3. Store in an airtight bottle in a refrigerator.

Makes half a cup of curry paste.

Note: Massaman is a Thai dish with Muslim roots. Massaman paste is strong in taste. Tofu takes to it like fish to water.

Bean Curd With French Beans And Hot Hoisin Sauce

Ingredients

200 g	firm bean curd (tofu)
250 g	French beans, halved
3 tbsp	hoisin sauce
1 tbsp	sesame oil (til ka tel)
1 inch	ginger, sliced
10	garlic cloves, chopped
1	medium onion, sliced
1 tbsp	red chilli sauce
1 tbsp	soy sauce
	Salt to taste

Method

1 Cut the bean curd into half-inch thick fingers.

2 Heat the sesame oil in a pan. Add the ginger and garlic and sauté for two minutes. Add the onion and sauté for another two minutes.

3 Add the hoisin sauce and red chilli sauce and mix. Add the French beans and mix again.

4 Add the bean curd, soy sauce and salt and toss gently till heated through.

5 Serve hot.

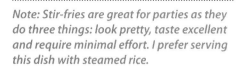

Note: Stir-fries are great for parties as they do three things: look pretty, taste excellent and require minimal effort. I prefer serving this dish with steamed rice.

Shahi Paneer

Ingredients

400 g	cottage cheese (paneer)
2	large onions, quartered
2 tbsp	oil
3	cloves (laung)
4-5	black peppercorns (kali mirch)
2	one-inch sticks cinnamon (dalchini)
1	bay leaf (tej patta)
2	green chillies, slit
1 tsp	ginger paste
1 tsp	garlic paste
¼ cup	cashew nut (kaju) paste
½ cup	yogurt (dahi)
½ cup	cream
	A pinch of saffron (kesar)
½ tsp	garam masala powder
	Salt to taste
¼ tsp	green cardamom (chhoti elaichi) powder

Method

1 Cut the *paneer* into half-inch wide and one-inch long pieces.

2 Boil the onions in a quarter cup of water. Drain and allow to cool. Grind the onions to a fine paste.

3 Heat the oil in a *kadai*; add the cloves, peppercorns, cinnamon and bay leaf and sauté till fragrant.

4 Add the green chillies and boiled onion paste and sauté for three to four minutes over a low heat so it does not get coloured. Add the ginger paste and garlic paste and continue to sauté for half a minute.

5 Add the cashew nut paste and sauté for another two minutes. Add the yogurt and sauté till the water from the yogurt gets absorbed. Stir in the cream, saffron, *garam masala* powder and salt to taste.

6 Add the *paneer* and stir gently to mix. Sprinkle green cardamom powder and serve hot.

Note: Paneer lovers will make a beeline for this dish so make sure you have sufficient quantities tucked away in the kitchen. Tastes great the following day too!

Handi Biryani

Ingredients

1½ cups	rice, soaked and drained
4	medium onions
	A few saffron (kesar) threads
	A few drops of kewra water
	Salt to taste
2-3	green cardamoms (chhoti elaichi)
1	black cardamom (badi elaichi)
2-3	cloves (laung)
1 inch	cinnamon (dalchini)
1	bay leaf (tej patta)
1	medium carrot, cut into ½-inch cubes
¼	medium cauliflower, separated into small florets
10-15	French beans, cut into ½-inch pieces
½ cup	shelled green peas
2 tbsp	oil + for deep-frying
½ tsp	caraway seeds (shahi jeera)
½ tbsp	ginger paste
½ tbsp	garlic paste
4-5	green chillies, chopped
1 tbsp	coriander (dhania) powder
1 tsp	turmeric powder (haldi)
1 tsp	red chilli powder
¾ cup	yogurt (dahi)
2	medium tomatoes, chopped
½ tsp	garam masala powder
2 tbsp	chopped fresh coriander (hara dhania)
2 tbsp	chopped fresh mint (pudina)
2 tbsp	ghee
1 inch	ginger, cut into thin strips

Note: Use flamboyance when you serve handi biryani... *open the seal with a little bit of drama as the aromas that escape foretell the wonderful contents... your effort in making it deserves all the accolades you will get.*

Method

1 Chop one onion and slice the rest. Soak the saffron in *kewra* water.

2 Cook the rice in four cups of boiling salted water with green cardamoms, black cardamom, cloves, cinnamon and bay leaf, until three-fourth done. Drain and set aside.

3 Mix together the carrot, cauliflower, French beans and peas and boil in three cups of salted water till three-fourth done. Drain and refresh under cold running water. Set aside.

4 Heat plenty of oil in a *kadai* and deep-fry the sliced onions till golden brown. Drain on absorbent paper and set aside.

5 Heat two tablespoons of oil in a thick-bottomed pan and add the caraway seeds. When they begin to change colour, add the chopped onions and sauté until golden brown.

6 Add the ginger paste, garlic paste and green chillies and stir. Add the coriander powder, turmeric powder, chilli powder and yogurt and mix well. Add the tomatoes and cook over a medium heat till the oil separates. Add the boiled vegetables and salt and mix well.

7 In a *handi*, arrange alternate layers of cooked vegetables and rice. Sprinkle the saffron-flavoured *kewra* water, *garam masala* powder, coriander leaves, mint leaves, fried onions and *ghee* in between the layers and on top. Make sure that you end with a rice layer topped with saffron and spices.

8 Cover and seal with aluminium foil or *roti* dough. Place the *handi* on a *tawa* and cook over a low heat for twenty minutes. Serve hot with *raita*.

Penne With Creamy Pesto And Cherry Tomatoes

Ingredients

200 g	penne (quill-shaped pasta), cooked
¼ cup	cream
20	cherry tomatoes
2 tbsp	olive oil
2	garlic cloves, sliced
5-6	black peppercorns (kali mirch), crushed
	Salt to taste

Pesto sauce

30-40	basil leaves (¾ cup) (tulsi ke patte)
4	garlic cloves
3 tbsp	pine nuts (chilgoze)
¼ cup	crumbled Parmesan cheese
5 tbsp	olive oil

Method

1 For the pesto sauce, grind together the basil leaves, garlic cloves, pine nuts and Parmesan cheese. Add the olive oil a little by little and grind till smooth.

2 Heat two tablespoons of olive oil in a pan. Add the sliced garlic and sauté till golden. Add the cherry tomatoes, pasta, peppercorns and salt and toss to mix.

3 Add the pesto sauce and toss. Add the cream and toss again till the pasta is coated with the sauce. Cook for one minute till heated through.

4 Serve hot.

Note: Pastas and parties are like salt and pepper: always together! This exotic pasta is one of the toppers on my list. Just make sure that the pine nuts are fresh and not rancid.

Laziz Tikka Masala

Ingredients

Chicken tikka

800 g	boneless chicken, cut into 1½-inch pieces
1 tsp	Kashmiri chilli powder
1 tbsp	lemon juice
	Salt to taste
4 tbsp	oil

Marinade

1 cup	drained (hung) yogurt (chakka)
1 tbsp	lemon juice
1 tbsp	ginger paste
1 tbsp	garlic paste
1 tsp	Kashmiri chilli powder
1 tsp	garam masala powder
2 tbsp	mustard oil (rai ka tel)

Onion-tomato masala

3	medium onions, chopped
4	medium tomatoes, chopped
3 tbsp	oil
½ tsp	cumin seeds (jeera)
7-8	garlic cloves, chopped
1 tsp	ginger paste
1 tsp	garlic paste
½ tsp	roasted cumin (bhuna jeera) powder
1½ tsp	coriander (dhania) powder

Gravy

2 tbsp	butter
1 tsp	ginger paste
1 tsp	garlic paste
¼ cup	tomato purée
1 cup	Onion-Tomato Masala (see alongside)
1 tsp	Kashmiri chilli powder
½ tsp	garam masala powder
2 tbsp	chopped fresh coriander (hara dhania)
1 tsp	roasted and crushed dried fenugreek leaves (kasuri methi)
¼ cup	cream
1 inch	ginger, cut into thin strips

Method

1 Mix together the chilli powder, lemon juice and salt. Add the chicken pieces and marinate for about thirty minutes.

2 For the marinade, mix together the drained yogurt, lemon juice, ginger and garlic pastes, chilli powder, *garam masala* powder and salt. Add the chicken pieces and mustard oil and mix well. Let the chicken marinate for about three hours in a refrigerator.

3 Thread the chicken onto skewers. Heat four tablespoons oil on a *tawa* and place the skewers on it. Cook, turning the skewers a few times, so that the chicken is cooked and evenly browned on all sides. Take the pieces off the skewers and place on a plate.

4 For the onion-tomato *masala*, heat the oil in a pan. Add the cumin seeds and when they begin to change colour, add the onions and sauté till well browned. Add the garlic and sauté till lightly browned. Add the ginger and garlic pastes and continue sautéing. Add the cumin powder and coriander powder and mix well.

Note: This is something that will cause a few raised eyebrows as it is likely that your guests will think that it has been ordered from a restaurant. You will need time to prepare it but believe me, the compliments are worth the effort.

5 Add the tomatoes and continue to sauté over a low heat till the tomatoes are completely cooked and the oil separates. Add salt and mix. Remove from heat and set aside.

6 For the gravy, heat the butter in a separate pan and add the ginger and garlic pastes and tomato purée and sauté for two minutes. Stir in half a cup of water and cook for two to three minutes. Add the chicken and onion-tomato *masala* and simmer till the gravy reduces a little. Adjust salt and add the chilli powder, *garam masala* powder and half the coriander leaves. Mix well and cook for two minutes.

7 Stir in the *kasuri methi* and cream. Remove from heat and serve hot, garnished with ginger strips and the remaining coriander leaves.

Kadai Prawns With Roasted Pepper Jam

Ingredients

400 g	large prawns (jheenga), peeled and deveined
4	dried red chillies, broken into bits
1 tsp	coriander seeds (dhania)
2 tbsp	lemon juice
	Salt to taste
3 tbsp	oil
1 tsp	carom seeds (ajwain)
1	medium onion, chopped
1 tsp	ginger-garlic paste
2	green chillies, chopped
½ tsp	roasted and crushed dried fenugreek leaves (kasuri methi)
¾ cup	Roasted Pepper Jam (see below)
2 tbsp	chopped fresh coriander (hara dhania)
½ tsp	garam masala powder

Roasted Pepper Jam

4	medium red capsicums (lal Shimla mirch), quartered
2	medium tomatoes, seeded and quartered
	Salt to taste
1 tsp	oil
3-4	garlic cloves, chopped
3 tbsp	cider vinegar (sirka)
2 tbsp	brown sugar
2 tsp	red chilli flakes

Note: The pepper jam can be prepared much in advance. No need to rush on the day of the party itself. The rest of the recipe is so simple that it is ready in a blink of an eye.

Method

1 To make the roasted pepper jam, preheat the oven to 180°C/350°F/Gas Mark 4.

2 Arrange the capsicums and tomatoes on a baking tray and sprinkle with salt. Bake for twenty to twenty-five minutes and set aside to cool. When completely cold, peel the capsicums and tomatoes and purée them in a blender.

3 Heat the oil in a non-stick pan; add the garlic and sauté for thirty seconds. Add the capsicum-tomato purée and cook for two minutes. Add the vinegar and bring to a boil. Lower the heat and add the brown sugar, chilli flakes and salt. Cook till reduced to half the quantity. Remove from heat and set aside.

4 Dry-roast the red chillies and coriander seeds. Cool and grind coarsely. Marinate the prawns in a mixture of the ground *masala*, lemon juice and salt for fifteen minutes.

5 Heat the oil in a pan; add the carom seeds. When they begin to change colour, add the onion and sauté till golden brown. Add the ginger-garlic paste and green chillies and sauté for thirty seconds.

6 Add the marinated prawns and stir-fry for a few minutes. Add one-fourth cup of water and cook till tender. Add the *kasuri methi* and mix well. Stir in the roasted pepper jam and mix till all the prawns are coated well.

7 Garnish with chopped fresh coriander and *garam masala* powder and serve hot.

Honey And Lemon Chicken On Rice

Ingredients

4	chicken breasts (100 g each), deboned
4 tbsp	honey (shahad)
2 tbsp	lemon juice
2 cups	brown rice, cooked
4 tbsp	olive oil
8-10	baby onions
2	medium carrots, thickly sliced
5-6	garlic cloves, crushed
1	inch ginger, finely chopped
1 tsp	chopped lemon rind (nimbu ka chilka)
	Salt to taste
2 tbsp	mustard (rai) paste
6 tbsp	orange juice
½ tsp	black pepper (kali mirch) powder
1 tsp	red chilli flakes
12	spinach (palak) leaves
½	medium yellow capsicum (pili Shimla mirch), diced
½	medium red capsicum (lal Shimla mirch), diced
½	medium green capsicum (hari Shimla mirch), diced
2 tbsp	butter
	A few sprigs of fresh parsley (ajmoda)

Method

1 Preheat the oven to 200ºC/400ºF/Gas Mark 6.

2 Heat half the olive oil in a pan. Add the baby onions and carrots and toss. Add the crushed garlic and sauté for two to three minutes.

3 In a bowl, mix together the ginger, lemon rind, salt, mustard paste, orange juice, pepper powder, half the chilli flakes, half the honey and the lemon juice. Marinate the chicken in the mixture for about fifteen minutes.

4 Spread the onion-carrot mixture in a baking tray. Place the marinated chicken with the marinade over the mixture. Place spinach leaves under each chicken breast. Pour the remaining honey on top and bake for fifteen minutes.

5 Heat the remaining olive oil in a pan. Add all the capsicums and sauté for a few minutes. Add the cooked brown rice and butter and toss to mix. Add salt and toss once again.

6 Remove the chicken from the oven and place on a plate. Glaze the chicken with the juices in the baking tray.

7 Transfer the vegetables from the baking tray onto a serving plate and place the chicken breasts on them. Serve the rice in a separate bowl. Sprinkle the remaining chilli flakes on both the chicken and rice. Garnish with parsley and serve hot.

Note: This platter will be greeted with a lot of 'oohs and aahs' as it looks good and is delicious to taste.

Chops Do Pyaaza

Ingredients

1 kg	lamb chops
4	large onions
10	tbsp oil
1 inch	cinnamon (dalchini)
10	green cardamoms (chhoti elaichi)
10	cloves (laung)
2 tsp	garlic paste
2 tsp	ginger paste
1 tbsp	coriander (dhania) powder
2 tsp	roasted cumin (bhuna jeera) powder
6 tbsp	yogurt (dahi), whisked
½ tsp	red chilli powder
	Salt to taste
½ tsp	garam masala powder

Note: Be very careful when buying the lamb chops. Choose only the freshest ones as the soul of the dish depends on the quality of the meat. Do pyaza means 'two onions' or rather 'double onions' which refers to the two ways in which the onions are chopped.

Method

1 Cut three onions in half vertically and slice them again into half rings. Chop the remaining onion.

2 Heat the oil in a thick-bottomed pan; add the sliced onions and sauté till golden-brown. Drain on absorbent paper.

3 Add the cinnamon, cardamoms and cloves to the oil remaining in the pan and stir-fry over a medium heat till fragrant. Add the lamb chops, a few at a time and stir-fry till brown. Drain and place them in a bowl.

4 Add the chopped onion to the same pan and sauté till golden-brown. Add the garlic and ginger pastes and sauté over a medium heat till the oil separates. Add the coriander powder and cumin powder and continue to sauté for half a minute.

5 Add the yogurt, one tablespoon at a time, and sauté till incorporated into the *masala*.

6 Add the lamb chops, one and a half cups of water, chilli powder and salt. Mix well and bring the mixture to a boil. Cover, lower the heat and cook for about forty-five minutes until the lamb is tender. If the dish is too dry, add half a cup of warm water.

7 Add the fried onions and *garam masala* powder and mix well. Adjust seasoning and continue to cook, uncovered, for another two to three minutes, stirring gently. Serve hot.

Chef's Tip: You can prepare the dish in advance and reheat just before serving.

Green Chilli Chicken

Ingredients

1 whole	chicken (800 g), cut into 1½-inch pieces
1 cup	small green chillies
3	green chillies, chopped
2	medium onions, quartered
10	garlic cloves
1½ inches	ginger, sliced
½ cup	chopped fresh coriander (hara dhania)
	Salt to taste
3 tbsp	oil
¾ tsp	cumin seeds (jeera)
¼ tsp	turmeric powder (haldi)
1 tsp	roasted cumin (bhuna jeera) powder
2 tsps	coriander (dhania) powder
1 tsp	garam masala powder

Method

1 Grind together the chopped green chillies, onions, garlic, ginger, chopped fresh coriander and salt. Marinate the chicken in this mixture for about half an hour.

2 Heat the oil in a wok or *kadai* and add the cumin seeds. When they begin to change colour add the turmeric powder. Add the marinated chicken and small green chillies and mix well. Add the cumin powder and coriander powder and stir to mix.

3 Add the *garam masala* powder and adjust the seasoning. Stir in half a cup of water, cover and cook over a medium heat for eight to ten minutes.

4 Lower the heat and cook for another eight to ten minutes or till the chicken is cooked. Serve hot.

Note: I confess that even I was surprised by the relative mildness of this dish! I expected it to be fiery hot with the amount of chillies used but it was not so. This is a piquant addition to your party menu!

Pan-fried Pomfret In Hot Black Bean Sauce

Ingredients

4	fish fillets (500-600 g) (preferably pomfret)
	Salt to taste
2 tbsp	malt vinegar (sirka)
2 tbsp	dark soy sauce
4 tbsp	cornflour
2 tbsp	oil + for deep-frying
2	spring onions, sliced
1 inch	ginger, chopped
2 tbsp	oyster sauce
2 tbsp	hot black bean sauce
7-8	black peppercorns (kali mirch), crushed
1	fresh red chilli, chopped
1 tsp	sugar
1	cup fish or chicken stock
2	stalks spring onion greens (hare pyaaz ke patte), chopped

Method

1. Mix together the salt, one tablespoon malt vinegar, one tablespoon dark soy sauce and three tablespoons cornflour in a bowl. Rub the mixture evenly over the pomfret fillets.

2. Heat plenty of oil in a wok and deep-fry the fillets for about a minute or till well done. Drain.

3. Heat two tablespoons of oil in a separate wok. Add the spring onions, ginger, oyster sauce, hot black bean sauce and remaining soy sauce and stir to mix. Add the peppercorns, red chilli, sugar and fish stock.

4. Mix the remaining cornflour with a quarter cup of water and remaining malt vinegar. Stir into the sauce and cook till the sauce thickens.

5. Place the fried fish on a serving plate and pour the sauce over. Garnish with spring onion greens and serve hot.

Note: This dish will provide an Oriental touch to your party with healthy white meat that is so much in demand now! Serve with steamed rice and extra spring onions.

Chicken Biryani

Ingredients

500 g	chicken on the bone, cut into 1½-inch pieces
1½ cups	sela (ukda Basmati) rice, soaked
1 tbsp	ginger paste
1 tbsp	garlic paste
1 tsp	green chilli paste
1 tbsp	coriander (dhania) powder
1 tbsp	roasted cumin (bhuna jeera) powder
1 tsp	garam masala powder
1 tsp	green cardamom (chhoti elaichi) powder
	Salt to taste
1 cup	yogurt (dahi)
3 tbsp	oil
1	bay leaf (tej patta)
4	cloves (laung)
2	green cardamoms (chhoti elaichi)
1	black cardamom (badi elaichi)
5 cups	chicken stock
	A few saffron threads (kesar)
1 tbsp	milk
1 tsp	caraway seeds (shahi jeera)
1 inch	ginger, cut into thin strips
2	medium onions, sliced and deep-fried
½ cup	chopped fresh mint (pudina)
2 tbsp	chopped fresh coriander (hara dhania)
1 tsp	kewra water
1 tsp	rose water

Method

1 Marinate the chicken in a mixture of ginger paste, garlic paste, green chilli paste, coriander powder, cumin powder, *garam masala* powder, cardamom powder, salt and yogurt for about half an hour.

2 Heat one tablespoon of oil in a pan. Add the bay leaf, cloves, green cardamoms and black cardamom and sauté for half a minute. Add the rice and sauté for a minute. Add the chicken stock and bring to a boil. Lower the heat and cook for eight to ten minutes or till the rice is three-fourths done. Drain and set aside.

3 Soak the saffron in the milk.

4 Heat the remaining oil in a thick-bottomed pan. Add the caraway seeds and sauté till fragrant. Add the marinated chicken and sauté for three to four minutes or till half cooked.

5 Remove the pan from the heat. Spread the rice over the chicken. Sprinkle the saffron-flavoured milk, ginger strips, fried onions, chopped fresh mint and coriander, *kewra* water and rose water over the rice. Cover and cook on *dum* for fifteen to twenty minutes over a low heat.

6 Serve hot with a *raita* of your choice.

Note: A biryani is a predictable dish at any party and why not? It is a hot favourite and will please all your non-vegetarian guests. Especially those who are not adventurous enough to try out new dishes.

Seafood Pad Thai

Ingredients

12	small prawns (jheenga), peeled and deveined
100 g	fish fillets, cut into 1-inch pieces
8-10	mussels or clams
200 g	flat noodles, boiled
3 tbsp	oil
5-6	spring onions, chopped
5-6	garlic cloves, chopped
1	medium green capsicum (hari Shimla mirch), cut into thin strips
	Salt to taste
1 tsp	soy sauce
2 tbsp	brown sugar
2	fresh red chillies, sliced diagonally
5-6	stalks spring onion greens (hare pyaaz ke patte), chopped
3 tbsp	roasted peanuts (bhuni moongphali), coarsely ground
1 tbsp	lemon juice
½ cup	bean sprouts (ankurit moong)

Method

1 Pat the prawns dry with an absorbent kitchen towel. Open the mussels or clam shells with a knife and scoop out the meat.

2 Heat the oil in a pan; add the onions, garlic, prawns, fish, mussels, capsicum and toss to mix.

3 Add the noodles, salt, soy sauce, brown sugar and toss once more.

4 Add the red chillies, spring onion greens and most of the roasted peanuts one after the other, tossing after each addition.

5 Transfer to a serving dish. Sprinkle the lemon juice and bean sprouts and top with the remaining roasted peanuts. Serve at once.

Chef's Tip: To boil the noodles, bring seven to eight cups of water to a boil in a large pan. Add the flat noodles and cook till al dente (cooked but firm to the bite). Drain and refresh in cold water. Spread on a plate to cool.

Note: Pad Thai or stir-fry is a popular Thai street food. I have dressed it up so that it is fit for a party!

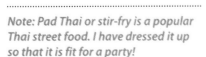

Grapes And Walnut Raita

Ingredients

25-30	green or red grapes, halved
¼ cup	walnut kernels (akhrot), chopped
2 cups	yogurt (dahi)
	Salt to taste
1½ tsp	sugar
½ tsp	roasted cumin (bhuna jeera) powder
2 tbsp	chopped fresh mint (pudina)
	A large pinch of red chilli powder

Method

1 Whisk the yogurt in a large bowl with salt, sugar and cumin powder.

2 Add the grapes, walnuts and mint and fold in gently. Place in a refrigerator to chill.

3 Sprinkle chilli powder and serve.

Note: Succulent grapes that look like green jewels, make this raita truly inviting. Serve in a large clear glass bowl for maximum effect.

Herb And Garlic Bread

1	French loaf (baguette)
1 tbsp	dried oregano
10-12	garlic cloves, finely chopped
100 g	butter

Method

1 Preheat the oven to 200°C/400°F/Gas Mark 6.

2 Soften the butter, add the oregano and garlic and mix well.

3 Cut the loaf into one-inch thick slices without cutting through. Spread the garlic butter generously between the slices. Wrap the loaf in aluminium foil and bake for fifteen minutes.

4 Separate the slices and serve warm.

Note: The secret of success of this bread is not to stint on the garlic. And be patient enough to bake it for the stipulated time for the flavours to seep through and through.

Eggless Pineapple Mousse

Ingredients

6 slices	tinned pineapple (ananas), at room temperature
2 tsp	unflavoured gelatine
½ tin	(200 g) sweetened condensed milk
3 tsp	lemon juice
250 g	cream
	A few drops of pineapple essence
	A few drops of edible yellow colour
1 tbsp	powdered sugar
	Glacé cherries, as required

Note: Making a mousse without eggs is possible! This mousse has great possibilities as a finale at a party: you can serve it in individual stemmed glasses or set it in a large flat dish and serve in squares or wedges, decorated with cream and cherries or other fresh fruits.

Method

1. Mix the gelatine with half a cup of water in a small pan. Cook over a low heat, stirring continuously, till it dissolves.

2. In a bowl, beat the condensed milk till light and creamy. In another bowl, mix lemon juice with half a cup of pineapple syrup from the tin.

3. Chop five slices of pineapple. Add the pineapple syrup and pineapple to the condensed milk.

4. Pour the gelatine solution into the condensed milk mixture stirring continuously. Freeze the mixture for half an hour till thick.

5. Remove from the freezer and beat till smooth. Fold in two hundred grams of cream and reserve the remaining cream for decoration.

6. Add the pineapple essence and yellow colour and beat well and put it back into the freezer for fifteen to twenty minutes.

7. Remove from freezer and beat again till smooth. Pour into a serving dish and freeze for one hour or till set.

8. Whip the reserved cream with the powdered sugar.

9. Remove the mousse from the freezer. Put the whipped cream into a piping bag fitted with a star nozzle and pipe rosettes on the surface of the mousse. Place a glacé cherry on each rosette and serve immediately.

Tiramisù

Ingredients

12 slices	chocolate sponge cake (175 g)
½ tbsp	unflavoured gelatine
1 cup	thick cream
½ cup	powdered sugar
3	egg yolks
¼ cup	sugar
2 tbsp +	
2 tsp	instant coffee powder
¾ cup	mascarpone cheese
	chocolate curls, to decorate

Method

1 Cut each slice of cake in half. Dissolve the gelatine in three tablespoons of hot water. Whip the cream with powdered sugar till stiff and set aside.

2 Whip the egg yolks with sugar and one tablespoon of water in a double-boiler, or in a heatproof bowl over a pan of simmering water, till the mixture forms thick ribbons. Set aside to cool.

3 Mix two teapoons of instant coffee powder in half a cup of water and soak the chocolate sponge fingers in this solution. Arrange half the sponge fingers in a layer at the bottom of a six-inch round spring-form tin.

4 Mix two tablespoons of instant coffee powder in one teaspoon of water. Add this along with mascarpone cheese and gelatine to the egg mixture and mix well. Fold in the whipped cream.

5 Pour half the mixture over the chocolate fingers. Arrange the remaining chocolate fingers over the coffee mixture and top with the remaining mixture and level the top. Place in a refrigerator till set.

6 Remove from the tin, cut into wedges and serve chilled, decorated with chocolate curls.

Note: It takes only a few essentials to get one of the most popular Italian desserts right. When literally translated it means 'pick me up' or to put it in a better way 'make me happier'!

Kesari Indrayani

Ingredients

20-25	small rosogollas
1½ litres	full cream milk
1 cup	fresh cream
¾ cup	sugar
	A few threads of saffron (kesar)
8-10	pistachios (pista)
½ cup	fresh pomegranate kernels (anar)
½ cup	mawa, grated
½ cup	almonds (badam), blanched and peeled

Method

1 Blanch the pistachios in boiling water. Drain, refresh, peel and slice.

2 Bring the milk to a boil, lower the heat and simmer till the milk reduces to half its original volume.

3 Add the cream, sugar and saffron and cook till the sugar dissolves.

4 Squeeze the *rosogollas* to remove excess syrup and place them in a bowl. Pour the milk-cream mixture over and set aside to cool. When completely cold, place in a refrigerator to chill.

5 To serve, place a few chilled *rosogollas* in each bowl. Sprinkle pistachios, pomegranate, grated *mawa* and almonds on top and serve at once.

Note: What I love about this dessert is that it looks and tastes superb and belies the simple method of preparation. It is also great to make when you have large numbers to entertain.

Mango And Coconut Ice Cream

Ingredients

2	medium ripe mangoes
1 cup	coconut milk
2 tbsp	grated coconut
2 tsp	lemon juice
1 cup	milk
3 tbsp	cornflour
½ cup	sugar
¼ tsp	salt
2	egg whites
½ cup	cream

Method

1 Peel the mangoes and purée the pulp with lemon juice in a blender.

2 Mix together the coconut milk and half the milk in a saucepan. Mix the cornflour with the remaining milk and add sugar and salt. Add to the coconut milk mixture and cook over a low heat, stirring continuously, until thick.

3 Stir in the grated coconut and set aside to cool. Add the mango purée and mix well. Pour into a bowl, cover tightly and place in the freezer until half frozen.

4 Beat the egg whites until soft peaks are formed. Whisk the cream till thick.

5 Transfer the mango mixture to another bowl. Fold in the beaten egg whites and mix until smooth. Fold in the cream and mix well.

6 Freeze the ice cream for three hours. Remove from the freezer and beat again till smooth. Return to the freezer until well frozen.

*Note: Mango in its myriad moods is always a winner! It marries well with coconut and this ice cream is a classic dessert that can make sweet memories. You can also freeze the mixture in **kulfi** moulds for easier serving.*

Mango Bhapa Doi With Citrus Fruit

Ingredients

1 tin	condensed milk (400 g)
1 cup	thick yogurt (dahi), whisked
½ cup	mango pulp
½ cup	milk
	A few peeled orange segments
	A few peeled sweet lime (mosambi) segments
	A few pomegranate kernels (anar)
	A small sprig of fresh mint (pudina)

Method

1 Pour the condensed milk into a bowl. Add the yogurt, mango pulp and milk and mix well. Transfer the mixture into a heatproof container.

2 Heat sufficient water in a steamer. Cover the container with aluminium foil and place in the steamer. Cover the steamer and steam for twenty to twenty-five minutes.

3 Cool and place in a refrigerator to set.

4 Unmould onto a serving plate. Arrange the orange and sweet lime segments in a decorative pattern all around. Top with a few pomegranate kernels. Place a small sprig of mint on top and serve chilled.

Note: I love making this deliciously simple dish during the mango season. The final colourful presentation always brings smiles when brought to the table.

Crème Brûlée

Ingredients

500 ml	cream
4	egg yolks
1	whole egg
1 cup +
1½ tbsp	sugar
½ tsp	vanilla essence
4 tbsp	Demerara sugar

Method

1 Heat the cream in a pan till it reaches boiling point. Set aside to cool.

2 Place the egg yolks and whole egg in a bowl; add all the sugar and mix. Cook in a double-boiler, or in a heatproof bowl over a pan of simmering water, till the sugar dissolves, making sure that the eggs do not scramble.

3 Add the egg mixture to the cream and mix well.

4 Preheat the oven to 180°C/350°F/Gas Mark 4.

5 Add the vanilla essence to the cream mixture and mix well. Strain the entire mixture into a separate bowl.

6 Pour the cream mixture into four ramekin moulds. Cover each mould with aluminium foil and pierce to allow the steam to escape. Pour some water into a deep baking tray. Place the moulds in the water bath and place the tray in the oven. Bake for twenty to twenty-five minutes.

7 Remove from oven, take the moulds out of the water bath and allow them to cool completely. Chill in the refrigerator.

8 Just before serving, sprinkle a tablespoon of Demerara sugar over the set custard in each of the moulds and caramelise the sugar with the torch.

9 Serve immediately.

Note: Crème brûlée literally means 'burnt cream'. To 'brûlée' means to caramelise the sugar topping, usually done with a small propane torch especially meant for kitchen use. In this dessert, the solid caramel topping creates a delightful textural contrast between the soft custard and brittle caramel.

Chef's Tip: A double-boiler is easily installed. Take a small vessel and pour some water in it. Allow it to come to a boil. Place the ingredients which need to be cooked or melted in another vessel which is larger in size. Place the larger vessel on the smaller one and allow the steam from the boiling water to cook/melt the ingredients.

Mango Cheesecake

Crust

8-10	bran biscuits or digestive biscuits
4 tbsp	butter

Filling

1 cup	skimmed milk
½ cup	condensed milk
1 tbsp	cornflour
1 tbsp	carrageenan (vegetarian gelatine)
1½ cups	skimmed milk yogurt (dahi), drained
2 cups	skimmed milk cottage cheese (paneer)
2 cups	mango pulp
½ tsp	mango essence
½ cup	sugar, powdered

Topping

1 tbsp	mango jelly crystals
1	mango, peeled and chopped

1 Crush the biscuits to a coarse powder and place in a bowl. Add the butter and mix well. Place the mixture in a six-inch round spring-form tin (loose-bottom tin) lined with greaseproof paper. Press the mixture lightly and place it in the refrigerator to set.

2 Heat the milk in a pan. Add the condensed milk and mix. Mix the cornflour with a little milk and add it to the hot milk. Cook, stirring continuously, till the mixture thickens. Set aside.

3 Mix the carrageenan in a little water and heat in the microwave for one minute. Remove and set aside.

4 Place the drained yogurt in a bowl. Add the paneer and whisk well. Add the mango pulp and mix again. Add the mango essence and the milk mixture and mix again. Add the powdered sugar and blend with a hand blender. Add the dissolved carrageenan and blend again.

5 Pour the mixture into the prepared tin over the biscuit layer. Refrigerate for two to three hours.

6 Dissolve the mango jelly crystals in a quarter cup of water, bring to a boil and cool.

7 Spread a layer of mango jelly over the set cheesecake. Chill until the jelly sets.

8 Remove from the spring-form tin and cut into eight wedges with a sharp knife dipped in hot water. Serve chilled, decorated with chopped mango.

....

Note: Cheesecake is something that does not require a lucky charm... contrary to popular belief! This recipe is a sure success and purely vegetarian.

Chef's Tip: A spring-form tin is a round shallow cake tin with a removable base.

Walnut Chocolate Fudge

Ingredients

½ cup	walnut halves (akhrot), finely chopped
100 g	dark chocolate, grated
4 tbsp	unsalted butter
400 g	condensed milk
½ cup	khoya/mawa, grated
½ tsp	vanilla essence

Method

1 Grease a seven-inch square baking tray.

2 Heat a pan; add the butter and allow it to melt. Add the chocolate and stir till it melts. Stir in the condensed milk and cook for two to three minutes.

3 Add the walnuts to the pan and mix. Add the grated *khoya*, vanilla essence and mix well.

4 Transfer the mixture to the greased tray and spread evenly. Cool in the refrigerator before cutting into pieces. Serve chilled.

Note: Chocolate is what makes the world go round for a number of people! Do make this sweet if chocolate is a favourite with your guests and remember to make extra as they will not mind carrying some home too!

Glossary

Baste ▸	Moisten with gravy or melted fat during cooking.
Beat ▸	Introduce air into a mixture, e.g. egg yolks or cake batter, by rotating it rapidly in a bowl, either with a spatula or an electric beater.
Blanch ▸	Immerse briefly in boiling water.
Deep-fry ▸	Fry in plenty of fat
Drain ▸	Remove excess liquid or fat from food usually with the help of a colander or by placing on absorbent paper.
Drizzle ▸	Pour liquid slowly in a thin stream over food e.g. vegetables with olive oil.
Dropping Consistency ▸	When a mixture like batter is too thick to pour but will fall from a spoon in lumps.
Dry-roast ▸	Heat/lightly fry, usually spices, on a griddle (tawa).
Dust ▸	Sprinkle lightly with flour or sugar.
Garnish ▸	Decorate food at the end of cooking.
Glaze ▸	Brush fat or liquid over food to give it a glossy look.
Grill/Broil ▸	Cook under or over direct heat by placing food on a metal grid.
Marinate ▸	Soak meat, fish etc., before cooking, in a mixture of spices and/or souring agents such as lemon juice or yogurt.
Parboil ▸	Partially cook by boiling briefly in water.
Purée ▸	Make a soft, smooth pulp of vegetables or fruit usually in a blender.
Refresh ▸	Run cold water over blanched food.
Sauté ▸	Fry quickly in a little hot oil.
Scorch ▸	Burn or become burnt at the edges.
Simmer ▸	Cook food gently in liquid just below boiling point.
Stir-fry ▸	Fry quickly over high heat in a lightly oiled pan (as in a wok) while stirring continuously.
Toss ▸	Mix ingredients in a quick, light way, till thoroughly blended.
Whisk ▸	Whip or beat ingredients to incorporate air and make light, e.g. egg whites, yogurt or cream.